WHY SHOULD YOU VOTE FOR THE DEMOCRATS IN THE 2020 ELECTIONS

HOW TO USE THIS BOOK?

IT'S EASY AS 1,2,3...

1
READ THIS BOOK

2
GIVE THIS BOOK TO EVERYONE YOU KNOW

3
VOTE FOR THE DEMOCRATS

DO THEY CARE ABOUT

EDUCATION

YES ⋮ NO

WINNER

DO THEY CARE ABOUT

★FAMILY VALUES

YES

NO

WINNER

DO THEY CARE ABOUT
BUDGET AND SPENDING

YES | NO

WINNER

DO THEY CARE ABOUT

HEALTH CARE

YES

NO

WINNER

DO THEY CARE ABOUT

ENVIRONMENT

YES   NO

WINNER

DO THEY CARE ABOUT

ENERGY

YES   NO

WINNER

DO THEY CARE ABOUT

IMMIGRATION

YES

NO

WINNER

DO THEY CARE ABOUT
FOREIGN RELATIONS

YES   NO

WINNER

DO THEY CARE ABOUT
LIBERTY

YES | NO

WINNER

DO THEY CARE ABOUT

COVID 19

YES

NO

WINNER

DO THEY CARE ABOUT
HOMELAND SECURITY

YES   NO

WINNER

DO THEY CARE ABOUT

CRIME

YES

NO

WINNER

DO THEY CARE ABOUT

★ ★ ★
CIVIL RIGHTS

YES  NO

✓

WINNER ✓

DO THEY CARE ABOUT

ECONOMY

YES NO

WINNER

DO THEY CARE ABOUT

OTHER ISSUES

YES   NO

WINNER

TOTAL WINS FOR THE DEMOCRATIC PARTY

15

I SHOULD VOTE FOR

WELL DONE! GO FOR IT!

NOTES

NOTES

NOTES

NOTES

Made in the USA
Monee, IL
05 February 2024

52958308R00015